The Book of **Bird Poems**

First published in Great Britain in 2024 by Laurence King, an imprint of The Orion Publishing Group Ltd, Carmelite House, 50 Victoria Embankment, London EC4Y 0DZ

An Hachette UK Company

10 9 8 7 6 5 4 3 2 1

Introduction © Ana Sampson 2024
Illustrations © Ryuto Miyake 2022, 2024

A CIP catalogue record for this book is available from the British Library.

ISBN (Hardback) 978 1 39962 563 0
ISBN (eBook) 978 1 39962 564 7

Origination by F1 Colour Ltd
Printed in China by C&C Offset Printing Co., Ltd.

www.laurenceking.com
www.orionbooks.co.uk

The Book of **Bird Poems**

Ryuto Miyake & Ana Sampson

Laurence King

Contents

Introduction

'The blue deep thou wingest,
And singing still dost soar, and soaring ever singest.'
Percy Bysshe Shelley

Imagine a day without birds.

It's a terrible thing to picture, wherever in the world you are and whatever birds can be seen from your window. The held-breath silence of an empty wood or the desolation of a bare coastline is not to be contemplated. Part of the reason that wild birds hold a special place in our hearts is because we live alongside them almost everywhere on earth.

Birds are busy, always. Superficially, we know much about their habits and drives, but to watch them in action is always to glance into a mysterious world, one that's bursting with activity. They are striving and feeding, hunting and wooing, bathing and conspiring, these little daughters of dinosaurs. Round and cheerful like the robin or graceful and balletic like the flamingo, infinitely varied and forever engaged in their urgent secret pursuits, it is no wonder that we are so fascinated by them. And perhaps there is a special relationship between the avian world and writers: who else, after all, will have spent so many hours gazing out of their windows?

Recently, my daughter and I rose early and ventured out into the nearby wood as dawn broke across the winter sky. (I'm not hardy enough to do this in summer, which would require a 4.30am alarm, but I could brave a January sunrise.) As the horizon lightened, little by little, the trees around us came alive. As well as the tick of a woodpecker, we heard the tumbling carols of the blackbirds, the insistent cheep of sparrows, the yodel of finches and the impudent sawing of the crows echoing around us.

How can we describe, in mere words, the sound of birdsong?

This is the task so many of the poets in this book set themselves, and I believe they come as close as fragile language can to that holy sound. We can see how closely they have watched their subjects to paint these portraits. Blake observes a lark whose 'little throat labours with inspiration, every feather / On throat and breast and wings vibrates', and Hardy's darkling thrush is aged, 'frail, gaunt, and small,/ In blast-beruffled plume', making his ecstatic hymn more moving still. Flora Cruft's night birds have 'lungs the size / of spider heads' from which they herald the dusk.

When birds sing, no matter how many times we have heard the sound before, it is astonishing. It can lift our spirits when we languish in the heart of darkness. I have included Adlestrop here – the beautiful, deservedly famous poem by Edward Thomas. Thomas never returned from the Western Front, but he left us his deathless words and the song of a long-gone blackbird, with the choirs of Oxfordshire and Gloucestershire rising behind it. It is an exquisite legacy.

Just as the dawn and dusk choirs punctuate our progress through the day, birds bind us to the changing seasons. The exhilarating babel of spring, when some return from wintering away and most look to nest and breed, can lift the most jaded of souls. The world comes alive, then, with their song and bustle, from the busy sparrows to Longfellow's returning stork. For many poets in the British Isles, tracing back centuries, the calls of the cuckoo and buzzing twitter of swallows ring in the summer.

As shadows lengthen and trees turn, the sight of migrating birds on the wing – like Yeats' swans at Coole – is a timeless reminder of the seasons' steady roll. The birds answer some deep and ancient pull, and an answering note is struck in us below, as we gather in our summer selves and turn our minds to wintering. Through the cold, dark months, those that stay continue to serenade us, though, and their song never fails to lift our hearts. For a moment when we lift our heads and hear them we, too, dip and soar and ride the wind. I hope these poems give you wings.

Ana Sampson

Pack, Clouds, Away, and Welcome Day

Thomas Heywood (c. 1574–1641)

Pack, clouds, away, and welcome day,
  With night we banish sorrow;
Sweet air blow soft, mount larks aloft
  To give my Love good-morrow!
Wings from the wind to please her mind
  Notes from the lark I'll borrow;
Bird, prune thy wing, nightingale sing,
  To give my Love good-morrow;
    To give my Love good-morrow
    Notes from them both I'll borrow.

Wake from thy nest, Robin-red-breast,
  Sing, birds, in every furrow;
And from each hill, let music shrill
  Give my fair Love good-morrow!
Blackbird and thrush in every bush,
  Stare, linnet, and cock-sparrow!
You pretty elves, amongst yourselves
  Sing my fair Love good-morrow;
    To give my Love good-morrow
    Sing, birds, in every furrow!

Ducks' Ditty

Kenneth Grahame (1859–1932)

All along the backwater,
Through the rushes tall,
Ducks are a-dabbling,
Up tails all!

Ducks' tails, drakes' tails,
Yellow feet a-quiver,
Yellow bills all out of sight
Busy in the river!

Slushy green undergrowth
Where the roach swim –
Here we keep our larder,
Cool and full and dim!

Everyone for what he likes!
We like to be
Heads down, tails up,
Dabbling free!

High in the blue above
Swifts whirl and call –
We are down a-dabbling
Up tails all!

The Lark's Song

William Blake (1757–1827)

Thou hearest the Nightingale begin the Song of Spring;
The lark sitting upon his earthly bed, just as the morn
Appears, listens silent, then springing from the waving
    Corn-field, loud
He leads the Choir of Day-trill, trill, trill, trill,
Mounting upon the wing of light into the Great Expanse,
Re-echoing against the lovely blue and shining heavenly
    Shell,
His little throat labours with inspiration, every feather
On throat and breast and wings vibrates with the
    effluence Divine.
All nature listens silent to him, and the awful Sun
Stands still upon the Mountain looking on this little Bird
With eyes of soft humility and wonder, love, and awe.

Azure and Gold

Amy Lowell (1874–1925)

April had covered the hills
  With flickering yellows and reds,
The sparkle and coolness of snow
  Was blown from the mountain beds.

Across a deep-sunken stream
  The pink of blossoming trees,
And from windless appleblooms
  The humming of many bees.

The air was of rose and gold
  Arabesqued with the song of birds
Who, swinging unseen under leaves,
  Made music more eager than words.

Of a sudden, aslant the road,
  A brightness to dazzle and stun,
A glint of the bluest blue,
  A flash from a sapphire sun.

Blue-birds so blue, 't was a dream,
  An impossible, unconceived hue,
The high sky of summer dropped down
  Some rapturous ocean to woo.

Such a colour, such infinite light!
  The heart of a fabulous gem,
Many-faceted, brilliant and rare.
  Centre Stone of the earth's diadem!

Centre Stone of the Crown of the World,
  'Sincerity' graved on your youth!
And your eyes hold the blue-bird flash,
  The sapphire shaft, which is truth.

Proud Songsters

Thomas Hardy (1840–1928)

The thrushes sing as the sun is going,
And the finches whistle in ones and pairs,
And as it gets dark loud nightingales
   In bushes
Pipe, as they can when April wears,
  As if all Time were theirs.

These are brand-new birds of twelve-months' growing,
Which a year ago, or less than twain,
No finches were, nor nightingales,
   Nor thrushes,
But only particles of grain,
  And earth, and air, and rain.

The Windhover

Gerard Manley Hopkins (1844–1889)

To Christ our Lord

I caught this morning morning's minion, king-
     dom of daylight's dauphin, dapple-dawn-drawn
        Falcon, in his riding
     Of the rolling level underneath him steady air,
        and striding
High there, how he rung upon the rein of a
        wimpling wing

In his ecstasy! then off, off forth on swing,
     As a skate's heel sweeps smooth on a bow-bend:
        the hurl and gliding
     Rebuffed the big wind. My heart in hiding

Stirred for a bird, – the achieve of, the mastery of
        the thing!
        Brute beauty and valour and act, oh, air, pride,
            plume, here
        Buckle! AND the fire that breaks from thee then,
            a billion
Times told lovelier, more dangerous, O my chevalier!

        No wonder of it: shéer plód makes plough down
            sillion
Shine, and blue-bleak embers, ah my dear,
        Fall, gall themselves, and gash gold-vermilion.

from The Cornish Chough

John Harris (1820–1884)

Will such a quiet bower
Be ever more my dower
In this rough region of perpetual strife?
I like a bird from home
Forward and backward roam;
But there is rest beneath the Tree of Life.

In this dark world of din,
Of selfishness and sin,
Help me, dear Saviour, on Thy love to rest;
That, having cross'd life's sea,
My shatter'd bark may be
Moor'd safely in the haven of the blest.

The Muse at this sweet hour
Hies with me to my bower
Among the heather of my native hill;
The rude rock-hedges here
And mossy turf, how dear!
What gushing song! how fresh the moors and still!

No spot of earth like thee,
So full of heaven to me,
O hill of rock, piled to the passing cloud!
Good spirits in their flight
Upon thy crags alight,
And leave a glory where they brightly bow'd.

I well remember now,
In boy-days on thy brow,
When first my lyre among thy larks I found,
Stealing from mother's side
Out on the common wide,
Strange Druid footfalls seem'd to echo round.

Dark Cornish chough, for thee
My shred of minstrelsy
I carol at this meditative hour,
Linking thee with my reed,
Grey moor and grassy mead,
Dear carn and cottage, heathy bank and bower.

Birds' Nests

John Clare (1793–1864)

How fresh the air the birds how busy now
In every walk if I but peep I find
Nests newly made or finished all and lined
With hair and thistle down and in the bough
Of little awthorn huddled up in green
The leaves still thickening as the spring gets age
The Pinks quite round and snug and closely laid
And linnets of materials loose and rough
And still hedge sparrow moping in the shade
Near the hedge bottom weaves of homely stuff
Dead grass and mosses green an hermitage
For secresy and shelter rightly made
And beautiful it is to walk beside
The lanes and hedges where their homes abide

Green Rain

Mary Webb (1881–1927)

Into the scented woods we'll go,
And see the blackthorn swim in snow.
High above, in the budding leaves,
A brooding dove awakes and grieves;
The glades with mingled music stir,
And wildly laughs the woodpecker.
When blackthorn petals pearl the breeze,
There are the twisted hawthorn trees
Thick-set with buds, as clear and pale
As golden water or green hail –
As if a storm of rain had stood
Enchanted in the thorny wood,
And, hearing fairy voices call,
Hung poised, forgetting how to fall.

Lines Written in Early Spring

William Wordsworth (1770–1850)

I heard a thousand blended notes,
While in a grove I sate reclined,
In that sweet mood when pleasant thoughts
Bring sad thoughts to the mind.

To her fair works did Nature link
The human soul that through me ran;
And much it grieved my heart to think
What man has made of man.

Through primrose tufts, in that sweet bower,
The periwinkle trailed its wreaths;
And 'tis my faith that every flower
Enjoys the air it breathes.

The birds around me hopped and played,
Their thoughts I cannot measure: —
But the least motion which they made,
It seemed a thrill of pleasure.

The budding twigs spread out their fan,
To catch the breezy air;
And I must think, do all I can,
That there was pleasure there.

From Heaven if this belief be sent,
If such be Nature's holy plan,
Have I not reason to lament
What man has made of man?

The Satin Bower-bird

C. J. Dennis (1876–1938)

Spare a bloom of blue, lady,
To adorn a bower.
A violet will do, lady –
Any azure flower.
Since we hold a dance to-day,
We would make our ball-room gay,
Where the scented grasses sway.
And the tall trees tower.

Beautiful but shy, lady,
Yesterday we came
Dropping from the sky, lady,
Flecks of golden flame
Golden flame and royal blue –
We have come to beg of you
Any scrap of heaven's hue
For our dancing game.

Spare us but a leaf, lady,
If our suit be spurned
We shall play the thief, lady,
When your back is turned;
Ravishing your garden plot
Of the choicest you have got –
Pansy or forget-me-not –
Counting it well earned.

Then, if some rare chance, lady,
Later should befall.
And you gain a glance, lady,
At our dancing hall,
You will find your blossoms there
'Mid our decorations where,
With a proud, patrician air,
We hold the Bushland Ball.

The Woods and Banks

W. H. Davies (1871–1940)

The woods and banks of England now,
　Late coppered with dead leaves and old,
Have made the early violets grow,
　And bulge with knots of primrose gold.
Hear how the blackbird flutes away,
　Whose music scorns to sleep at night:
Hear how the cuckoo shouts all day
　For echoes – to the world's delight:
Hullo, you imp of wonder, you –
　Where are you now, cuckoo? Cuckoo?

Cuckoo

Anon

Sumer is icumen in,
Loud sing cuckoo!
Groweth seed and bloweth mead
And springeth the wood now.
Sing cuckoo!

Ewe bleateth after lamb,
Cow loweth after calf,
Bullock starteth, buck farteth,
Merry sing cuckoo!

Cuckoo, cuckoo!
Well singest thou cuckoo,
Nor cease thou never now!

Sing cuckoo now, sing cuckoo!
Sing cuckoo, sing cuckoo now!

Meadowlarks

Sara Teasdale (1884–1933)

In the silver light after a storm,
Under dripping boughs of bright new green,
I take the low path to hear the meadowlarks
Alone and high-hearted as if I were a queen.
What have I to fear in life or death
Who have known three things: the kiss in the night,
The white flying joy when a song is born,
And meadowlarks whistling in silver light.

The Birds of Paradise

John Peale Bishop (1892–1944)

I have seen the Birds of Paradise
Afloat in the heavy noon,
Their irised plumes, their trailing gold,
Their crested heads, like flames grown cold;
They rose and vanished soon.

Strange dust is blown into mine eyes;
I doubt I shall ever see
Their lightly lifted forms again,
Their burning plumes of holy grain,
And this is grief to me.

Humming-bird

D. H. Lawrence (1885–1930)

I can imagine, in some otherworld
Primeval-dumb, far back
In that most awful stillness, that only gasped
    and hummed,
Humming-birds raced down the avenues.

Before anything had a soul,
While life was a heave of Matter, half inanimate,
This little bit chipped off in brilliance
And went whizzing through the slow, vast,
    succulent stems.

I believe there were no flowers then,
In the world where the humming-bird flashed
    ahead of creation.
I believe he pierced the slow vegetable veins with
    his long beak.

Probably he was big
As mosses, and little lizards, they say, were once big.
Probably he was a jabbing, terrifying monster.

We look at him through the wrong end of the long
    telescope of Time,
Luckily for us.

Adlestrop

Edward Thomas (1878–1917)

Yes, I remember Adlestrop –
The name, because one afternoon
Of heat the express-train drew up there
Unwontedly. It was late June.

The steam hissed. Someone cleared his throat.
No one left and no one came
On the bare platform. What I saw
Was Adlestrop – only the name

And willows, willow-herb, and grass,
And meadowsweet, and haycocks dry,
No whit less still and lonely fair
Than the high cloudlets in the sky.

And for that minute a blackbird sang
Close by, and round him, mistier,
Farther and farther, all the birds
Of Oxfordshire and Gloucestershire.

Flamingo

John McCullough (b. 1978)

We prefer shallow water,
gathering in hundreds at night clubs
by the shore. The powder cakes
we bring say EAT ME and we do,
gobbling up beakfuls till our heads turn
upside-down. We don't know
how Sia and Audrey Hepburn joined us,
pirouetting across the floor. And who
invited the clouds? We don't mind.
Our origin is in fire. We are invincible,
even if we're imaginary figures
in some Red King's dream, even if
we may be losing it, may in fact just be me
standing on one perilous leg beside
the speaker, waiting for the rain to stop.

Landscape with Vultures

Pascale Petit (b. 1953)

The morning was almost over
when I came to Rajbhera Meadow
where hundreds of vultures had gathered.
They held up their wings, fanning the feathers
as if to say aren't we beautiful?
Or drank from the waterhole, or launched themselves
into the air after a run-up like a plane,
to land on a branch just above my head,
silhouetted against the sky like long-necked gods –
griffons from other worlds, death-eaters.
There is so much ugliness on this earth
but they should not be loathed for the way
they plunge their heads into corpses.
I wanted to be brave as them,
to plunge my face in the maggots and gore
and eat until nothing was left
except shining white ribs.
And here they were resting after work, getting on
    with their lives –
perhaps gossiping, or courting, or just
letting the sun worship each vane of their feathers.
I could see the breeze stir the soft grey down
on their breasts as if it loved them.

The meadow was enchanted
with its hazy backdrop of Bandhavgarh Fort
on its sacred plateau laced with their nests,
and I did not want to leave.
I thought about what happens
after death, how our souls might gather
on some shimmering plain after our descent
    from the ether,
the whirr of our wings as we perch on the tree
    of knowledge
staring past humans.
It was as if the carcasses of my life
were purged
just for that half hour
and I was allowed to see a volt of vultures –
some endangered, some rare, for there were
    Egyptians there,
Kings, Himalayans, and the Indian –
who had all soared in the stratosphere,
birds that can overcome the smell of fear
that must linger on a kill
to be digested by sky-beings.
I wanted to gobble up the poison of the world
and squirt it out in white splatters like summer snow,
then rise
in the alchemical light, clean as the moment of my birth
when the midwife washed my mother's scat from
    my skin.

The Ostrich

Mary E. Wilkins Freeman (1852–1930)

The ostrich is a silly bird,
With scarcely any mind.
He often runs so very fast,
He leaves himself behind.

And when he gets there, he has to stand
And hang about all night,
Without a blessed thing to do
Until he comes in sight.

The Three Ravens

Anon

There were three ravens sat on a tree,
  Down a down, hay down, hay down.
There were three ravens sat on a tree,
  With a down,
There were three ravens sat on a tree,
They were as black as they might be.
  With a down derry, derry, derry, down, down.

The one of them said to his mate,
"Where shall we our breakfast take?"

"Down in yonder greene field,
There lies a knight slain under his shield.

"His hounds they lie down at his feet,
So well they can their master keep.

"His hawks they fly so eagerly,
There's no fowl dare him come nigh."

Down there comes a fallow doe,
As great with young as she might go.

She lift up his bloody head
And kissed his wounds that were so red.

She got him up upon her back
And carried him to earthen lake.

She buried him before the prime;
She was dead herself ere even-song time.

God send every gentleman
Such hawks, such hounds, and such a leman.*

lover, sweetheart

'Repeat That, Repeat'

Gerard Manley Hopkins (1844–1889)

Repeat that, repeat,
Cuckoo, bird, and open ear wells, heart-springs,
    delightfully sweet,
With a ballad, with a ballad, a rebound
Off trundled timber and scoops of the hillside ground,
    hollow hollow hollow ground:
The whole landscape flushes on a sudden at a sound.

The Condor

Michael Hogan (b. 1943)

Dark and lugubrious, his eyes
signify no intent beyond brooding.
All day he has been posed on thermals
as if the land would rise like a hand
and say: Blessings! Blessings!
Observant as a child who watches
the sidewalk for a dollar
dropped by chance along the way to school.
He waits. The dollar's never there.
It is a story like the one they tell prisoners
of a world outside the walls to keep them
simple with hope.

Now he's passed the rift valley
empty of game and descends
smooth as a spent bullet to the Bay.
He feeds there on salmon spilled
by the fishing boats.
It is always less than he wanted.
He dreams of a freshly killed goat
on a grassy hill near Monterey,
a calf, a yearling torn by rocks
or the teeth of wild dogs.
But it is always something less.
Today salmon. Tomorrow a rabid skunk,

The Apache said the bird made thunder
by beating its wings. The Apache said
lightning was born on the condor's eyes.
I tell my son the old legends
but think instead of losses. Think of the doomed
Irish days of my grandfather and the miles
he drifted; his eyes red after a fifth of Jameson
as this great lost searcher's looking out at a world.
Always one which gave less than the dreams.
But he told me the legends. How there
was once a people whose poetry
thundered on Tara's hills, whose eyes flashed lightning.
When the world was young
and no man could measure the breadth of a life.

It was before the factories, before the wife
dead with the third child and the child stillborn.
It was before the friends imprisoned, the dole,

the immigration. I sometimes think, he said,

We call the condor an endangered species
and like the sound of that captured phrase.
And the condor, his wings transcendent
as an old memory beat: Alexander! Alexander!
With no other worlds to conquer.

from **Speak, Parrot**

John Skelton (1463–1529)

Parrot, Parrot, Parrot, pretty popinjay!
With my beak I can pick my little pretty toe.
My delight is solace, pleasure, disport, and play;
Like a wanton, when I will, I reel to and fro:
Parrot can say *Caesar, ave* also;
But Parrot hath no favour to Esebon:
Above all other birds, set Parrot alone.

The Kingfisher

W. H. Davies (1871–1940)

It was the Rainbow gave thee birth,
And left thee all her lovely hues;
And, as her mother's name was Tears,
So runs it in my blood to choose
For haunts the lonely pools, and keep
In company with trees that weep.
Go you and, with such glorious hues,
Live with proud peacocks in green parks;
On lawns as smooth as shining glass,
Let every feather show its marks;
Get thee on boughs and clap thy wings
Before the windows of proud kings.
Nay, lovely Bird, thou art not vain;
Thou hast no proud, ambitious mind;
I also love a quiet place
That's green, away from all mankind;
A lonely pool, and let a tree
Sigh with her bosom over me.

The Eagle

Alfred, Lord Tennyson (1809–1892)

He clasps the crag with crooked hands;
Close to the sun in lonely lands,
Ring'd with the azure world, he stands.

The wrinkled sea beneath him crawls;
He watches from his mountain walls,
And like a thunderbolt he falls.

The Dalliance of the Eagles

Walt Whitman (1819–1892)

Skirting the river road, (my forenoon walk, my rest,)
Skyward in air a sudden muffled sound, the dalliance
    of the eagles,
The rushing amorous contact high in space together,
The clinching interlocking claws, a living, fierce,
    gyrating wheel,
Four beating wings, two beaks, a swirling mass tight
    grappling,
In tumbling turning clustering loops, straight
    downward falling,
Till o'er the river pois'd, the twain yet one, a
    moment's lull,
A motionless still balance in the air, then parting,
    talons loosing,
Upward again on slow-firm pinions slanting, their
    separate diverse flight,
She hers, he his, pursuing.

Goldfinches

John Keats (1795–1821)

Sometimes goldfinches one by one will drop
From low hung branches: little space they stop;
But sip, and twitter, and their feathers sleek;
Then off at once, as in a wanton freak:
Or perhaps, to show their black and golden wings,
Pausing upon their yellow flutterings.

Requiescat

Charlotte Mew (1869–1928)

Your birds that call from tree to tree
    Just overhead, and whirl and dart,
Your breeze fresh-blowing from the sea,
    And your sea singing on, Sweetheart.

Your salt scent on the thin sharp air
    Of this grey dawn's first drowsy hours,
While on the grass shines everywhere
    The yellow starlight of your flowers.

At the road's end your strip of blue
    Beyond that line of naked trees –
Strange that we should remember you
    As if you would remember these!

As if your spirit, swaying yet
    To the old passions, were not free
Of spring's wild magic, and the fret
    Of the wilder wooing of the sea!

What threat of old imaginings,
    Half-haunted joy, enchanted pain,
Or dread of unfamiliar things
    Should ever trouble you again?

Yet you would wake and want, you said,
    The little whirr of wings, the clear
Gay notes, the wind, the golden bed
    Of the daffodil: and they are here!

Just overhead, they whirl and dart
    Your birds that call from tree to tree,
Your sea is singing on – Sweetheart,
    Your breeze is blowing from the sea.

Beyond the line of naked trees
    At the road's end, your stretch of blue –
Strange if you should remember these
    As we, ah! God! remember you!

from Turkey-cock

D. H. Lawrence (1885–1930)

Turkey-cock, turkey-cock,
Are you the bird of the next dawn?

Has the peacock had his day, does he call in vain,
      screecher, for the sun to rise?
The eagle, the dove, and the barnyard shouter, do they
      call in vain, trying to wake the morrow?
And do you await us, wattled father, Westward?
Will your yell do it?

Take up the trail of the vanished American
Where it disappeared at the foot of the crucifix.
Take up the primordial pride,
The more than human, dense magnificence,
And disdain, and indifference, and onrush; and pry open
      the new day with them.

Is the East a dead letter, and Europe moribund?
But those sumptuous, dead, feather-lustrous Aztecs,
      Amerindians,
In all the sombre splendor of their red blood,
Stand under the dawn, half-godly, awaiting the cry
      of the turkey-cock?

Swallows

Kathleen Jamie (b. 1962)

I wish my whole battened
heart were a property
like this, with swallows
in every room – so at ease

they twitter and preen
from the picture frames
like an audience in the gods
before an opera

and in the mornings
wheel above my bed
in a mockery of pity
before winging it

up the stairwell
to stream out into light

from The Rime of the Ancient Mariner

Samuel Taylor Coleridge (1772–1834)

With sloping masts and dipping prow,
As who pursued with yell and blow
Still treads the shadow of his foe,
And forward bends his head,
The ship drove fast, loud roared the blast,
And southward aye we fled.

And now there came both mist and snow,
And it grew wondrous cold:
And ice, mast-high, came floating by,
As green as emerald.

And through the drifts the snowy clifts
Did send a dismal sheen:
Nor shapes of men nor beasts we ken—
The ice was all between.

The ice was here, the ice was there,
The ice was all around:
It cracked and growled, and roared and howled,
Like noises in a swound!

At length did cross an Albatross,
Thorough the fog it came;
As if it had been a Christian soul,
We hailed it in God's name.

It ate the food it ne'er had eat,
And round and round it flew.
The ice did split with a thunder-fit;
The helmsman steered us through!

And a good south wind sprung up behind;
The Albatross did follow,
And every day, for food or play,
Came to the mariner's hollo!

In mist or cloud, on mast or shroud,
It perched for vespers nine;
Whiles all the night, through
    fog-smoke white,
Glimmered the white Moon-shine.

In the Fields

Charlotte Mew (1869–1928)

Lord, when I look at lovely things which pass,
    Under old trees the shadow of young leaves
Dancing to please the wind along the grass,
    Or the gold stillness of the August sun on the
    August sheaves;
Can I believe there is a heavenlier world than this?
    And if there is
Will the strange heart of any everlasting thing
    Bring me these dreams that take my breath away?
They come at evening with the home-flying rooks and
    the scent of hay,
    Over the fields. They come in Spring.

Yellow Penguin

Olga Dermott-Bond

Strange pale penguin: rare yellow and white bird
discovered among king penguins in Atlantic
– The Guardian, 25th February 2021

Instead of black wellies or waders
he is dressed in ballet pumps
and a dazzling cravat, overdressed
for the occasion of the Antarctic.

A fragile daisy who needs the cold
to bloom, his round belly is spilled
with a surprise of yolk, then custard,
smoothing to primrose, then snow –

The others are dressed in leather,
have inherited thick skin, deep tread,
yet his sides are slippery with oyster-
light, a gorgeous hiccup

                    in the genetic loop.

I can only watch while the glacier inside
my daughter calves into something even
more extraordinary, bright – I want
to tell her that one distant day somebody

will discover the exotic creature they are,
no need to hide underneath a black hoodie;
how they'll glow then, in their thin-skinned
difference,
                    exactly how he was hatched.

The Wild Swans at Coole

W. B. Yeats (1865–1939)

The trees are in their autumn beauty,
The woodland paths are dry,
Under the October twilight the water
Mirrors a still sky;
Upon the brimming water among the stones
Are nine-and-fifty swans.

The nineteenth autumn has come upon me
Since I first made my count;
I saw, before I had well finished,
All suddenly mount
And scatter wheeling in great broken rings
Upon their clamorous wings.

I have looked upon those brilliant creatures,
And now my heart is sore.
All's changed since I, hearing at twilight,
The first time on this shore,
The bell-beat of their wings above my head,
Trod with a lighter tread.

Unwearied still, lover by lover,
They paddle in the cold
Companionable streams or climb the air;
Their hearts have not grown old;
Passion or conquest, wander where they will,
Attend upon them still.

But now they drift on the still water,
Mysterious, beautiful;
Among what rushes will they build,
By what lake's edge or pool
Delight men's eyes when I awake some day
To find they have flown away?

Lights and Shadows

Sarah Doyle

We stood some minutes watching the swallows
that flew about restlessly, and flung their shadows
upon the sunbright walls of the old building;
the shadows glanced and twinkled, interchanged
and crossed each other, expanded and shrunk up,
appeared and disappeared every instant, seeming
more like living things than the birds themselves.
The sun shone so brightly, with such a fierce light,
that there was even something like the purity
of one of nature's own grand spectacles. Rocks
glittered in the sunshine, distant hills were visible,
the evening sun was now sending a glorious light.
Islanded with sunshine, bathed in golden light,
my heart danced while the sun was yet shining.

Le Jardin

Oscar Wilde (1854–1900)

The lily's withered chalice falls
Around its rod of dusty gold,
And from the beech-trees on the wold
The last wood-pigeon coos and calls.

The gaudy leonine sunflower
Hangs black and barren on its stalk,
And down the windy garden walk
The dead leaves scatter, – hour by hour.

Pale privet-petals white as milk
Are blown into a snowy mass:
The roses lie upon the grass
Like little shreds of crimson silk.

Something Told the Wild Geese

Rachel Field (1894–1942)

Something told the wild geese
  It was time to go.
Though the fields lay golden
  Something whispered, – 'Snow.'

Leaves were green and stirring,
  Berries, lustre-glossed,
But beneath warm feathers
  Something cautioned, – 'Frost.'

All the sagging orchards
  Steamed with amber spice,
But each wild breast stiffened
  At remembered Ice.

Something told the wild geese
  It was time to fly, –
Summer sun was on their wings,
  Winter in their cry.

from To a Skylark

Percy Bysshe Shelley (1792–1822)

Hail to thee, blithe Spirit!
  Bird thou never wert,
That from Heaven, or near it,
  Pourest thy full heart
In profuse strains of unpremeditated art.

Higher still and higher
  From the earth thou springest
Like a cloud of fire;
  The blue deep thou wingest,
And singing still dost soar, and soaring ever singest.

In the golden light'ning
  Of the sunken sun,
O'er which clouds are bright'ning,
  Thou dost float and run,
Like an unbodied joy whose race is just begun.

The pale purple even
  Melts around thy flight;
Like a star of Heaven,
  In the broad daylight
Thou art unseen, but yet I hear thy shrill delight,

Teach me half the gladness
  That thy brain must know,
Such harmonious madness
  From my lips would flow
The world should listen then – as I am listening now.

A Flaw

Michael Field

To give me its bright plumes, they shot a jay:
On the fresh jewels, blood! Oh, sharp remorse!
The glittering symbols of the little corse
I buried where the wood was noisome, blind,
Praying that I might nevermore betray
The universe, so whole within my mind.

The Sand-hill Crane and Other Wild Fowl of Mexico

Isaac McLellan (1806–1899)

The sand-hill crane hath winter home
In this serene, delicious clime;
Great flocks are ever in the air,
As high the azure vault they climb.
Where fields are open they are seen,
Cluster'd in dignified array,
Watching your step, with outstretch'd neck,
Or on the wing – a cloud of gray.

Fairest of all this feather'd tribe
Is great white crane, the whooping crane,
The wariest fowl of earth or air
That haunts the pool or sweep the plain.
Sometimes in zenith you behold
Their floating forms like specks of down,
In circles long, in spiral lines,
Sending their bugle-clamors down;
Sometimes commix'd with duskier cranes,
You see them pass in phalanx slow,
Keeping time-stroke with flapping wing,
Their plumage shining like the snow.

Autumn Birds

John Clare (1793–1864)

The wild duck startles like a sudden thought
And heron slow as if it might be caught.
The flopping crows on weary wings go by
And grey beard jackdaws noising as they fly.
The crowds of starnels wiz and hurry by
And darken like a cloud the evening sky.
The larks like thunder rise and study round
Then drop and nestle in the stubble ground.
The wild swan hurries high and noises loud
With white necks peering to the evening cloud.
The weary rooks to distant woods are gone;
With length of tail the magpie winnows on
To neighbouring tree and leaves the distant crow
While small birds nestle in the hedge below.

Night Birds

Flora Cruft

Walking in the garden, pulling bluebells
through arthritic fingers,

you tell me about the dusk chorus, how some
birds sing their loudest as the sun beds down.

We can hear them getting ready,
drawing air through their bills

down into lungs the size
of spider heads, air sacs

the bellows that inflate, deflate,
as tympanums vibrate.

One solitary note comes, then another,
bound to meet in flight.

Bird words collide like
blind arms embracing.

This is what we ageing creatures do:
drive our voices into the world

ink the sky with sound,
as night moves over the bluebells

searching for its place to be born.

from Paradise Lost

John Milton (1608–1674)

Meanwhile the tepid caves, and fens, and shores,
Their brood as numerous hatch, from the egg that soon
Bursting with kindly rupture forth disclosed
Their callow young; but feather'd soon and fledge
They summ'd their pens; and, soaring the air sublime,
With clang despised the ground, under a cloud
In prospect; there the eagle and the stork
On cliffs and cedar tops their eyries build:
Part loosely wing the region, part more wise
In common, ranged in figure, wedge their way,
Intelligent of seasons, and set forth
Their aery caravan, high over seas
Flying, and over lands, with mutual wing
Easing their flight; so steers the prudent crane
Her annual voyage, borne on winds; the air
Floats as they pass, fann'd with unnumber'd plumes:
From branch to branch the smaller birds with song
Solaced the woods, and spread their painted wings
Till even; nor then the solemn nightingale
Ceased warbling, but all night tuned her soft lays:
Others, on silver lakes and rivers, bathed
Their downy breast; the swan with arched neck,
Between her white wings mantling proudly, rows
Her state with oary feet; yet oft they quit

The dank, and rising on stiff pennons, tower
The mid äerial sky: Others on ground
Walk'd firm; the crested cock whose clarion sounds
The silent hours, and the other whose gay train
Adorns him, colour'd with the florid hue
Of rainbows and starry eyes.

Sunset Wings

Dante Gabriel Rossetti (1828–1882)

To-night this sunset spreads two golden wings
Cleaving the western sky;
Winged too with wind it is, and winnowings
Of birds; as if the day's last hour in rings
Of strenuous flight must die.
Sun-steeped in fire, the homeward pinions sway
Above the dovecote-tops;
And clouds of starlings, ere they rest with day,
Sink, clamorous like mill-waters, at wild play,
By turns in every copse:
Each tree heart-deep the wrangling rout receives,–
Save for the whirr within,
You could not tell the starlings from the leaves;
Then one great puff of wings, and the swarm heaves
Away with all its din.

Even thus Hope's hours, in ever-eddying flight,
To many a refuge tend;
With the first light she laughed, and the last light
Glows round her still, who natheless in the night
At length must make an end.
And now the mustering rooks innumerable
Together sail and soar,
While for the day's death, like a tolling knell,
Unto the heart they seem to cry, Farewell,
No more, farewell, no more!
Is Hope not plumed, as 'twere a fiery dart?
And oh! thou dying day,
Even as thou goest must she too depart,
And Sorrow fold such pinions on the heart
As will not fly away?

To the Mocking-bird

Richard Henry Wilde (1789–1847)

Winged mimic of the woods! thou motley fool!
Who shall thy gay buffoonery describe?
Thine ever ready notes of ridicule
Pursue thy fellows still with jest and gibe.
Wit, sophist, songster, Yorick of thy tribe,
Thou sportive satirist of Nature's school,
To thee the palm of scoffing we ascribe,
Arch-mocker and mad Abbot of Misrule!
For such thou art by day – but all night long
Thou pourest a soft, sweet, pensive, solemn strain,
As if thou didst in this thy moonlight song
Like to the melancholy Jacques complain,
Musing on falsehood, folly, vice, and wrong,
And sighing for thy motley coat again.

The Humming-bird

Mary Botham Howitt (1799–1888)

The Humming-bird! The Humming-bird,
So fairy-like and bright;
It lives among the sunny flowers,
A creature of delight!

In the radiant islands of the East,
Where fragrant spices grow,
A thousand thousand Humming-birds
Go glancing to and fro.

Like living fires they flit about,
Scarce larger than a bee,
Among the broad Palmetto leaves,
And through the Fan-palm tree.

And in those wild and verdant woods
Where stately Moras tower,
Where hangs from branching tree to tree
The scarlet Passion-flower;

Where on the mighty river banks,
La Plate or Amazon,
The Cayman like an old tree trunk,
Lies basking in the sun;

There builds her nest, the Humming-bird
Within the ancient wood,
Her nest of silky cotton down,
And rears her tiny brood.

She hangs it to a slender twig,
Where waves it light and free,
As the Campanero tolls his song,
And rocks the mighty tree.

All crimson in her shining breast,
Like to the red, red rose;
Her wing is the changeful green and blue
That the neck of the Peacock shews.

Thou happy, happy Humming-bird,
No winter round thee lowers;
Thou never saw'st a leafless tree,
Nor land without sweet flowers:

A reign of summer joyfulness
To thee for life is given;
Thy food the honey from the flower,
Thy drink, the dew from heaven!

How glad the heart of Eve would be,
In Eden's glorious bowers,
To see the first, first Humming-bird
Among the first spring-flowers.

Among the rainbow butterflies,
Before the rainbow shone;
One moment glancing in her sight,
Another moment, gone!

Thou little shining creature,
God saved thee from the Flood,
With the Eagle of the mountain land,
And the Tiger of the wood!

Who cared to save the Elephant,
He also cared for thee;
And gave those broad lands for thy home,
Where grows the Cedar-tree!

Swift by Your Side

Dom Conlon

Circle as you sleep, my love
and drift upon your dreams.
Ruling from the clouds, my love
is simpler than it seems.

Be queen above the world, my love
be the king who's free to fly.
Let the wealth within your wings, my love
be scattered in the sky.

The kingdom of your eye, my love
is measured by the sun.
The journey to my heart, my love
begins when that is done.

I hear your piper's call, my love
the poetry of tears.
I'll follow where you lead, my love
as months turn into years.

And when we go to ground, my love
when all our wings are old.
We'll gaze up to the blue, my love
and count our words of gold.

Winter Bird

Katherine Mansfield (1888–1923)

My bird, my darling,
Calling through the cold of afternoon –
Those round, bright notes,
Each one so perfect
Shaken from the other and yet
Hanging together in flashing clusters!
'The small soft flowers and the ripe fruit
All are gathered.
It is the season now of nuts and berries
And round, bright, flashing drops
In the frozen grass.'

That's What We'd Do

Mary Mapes Dodge (1831–1905)

If you were an owl,
And I were an owl,
And this were a tree,
   And the moon came out,
I know what we'd do.
We would stand, we two,
On a bough of the tree;
You'd wink at me,
And I'd wink at you;
That's what we'd do,
   Beyond a doubt.
I'd give you a rose
For your lovely nose,
And you'd look at me
   Without turning about.
I know what we'd do
(That is, I and you);
Why, you'd sing to me,
And I'd sing to you;
That's what we'd do,
   When the moon came out.

Sweet Suffolk Owl

Thomas Vautor

Sweet Suffolk owl, so trimly dight,
With feathers like a lady bright,
Thou sing'st alone, sitting by night:
Te-whit, te-whoo …
Thy note, that forth so freely rolls,
With shrill command the mouse controls,
And sings a dirge for dying souls:
Te-whit, te-whoo …

The Arctic Tern's Prayer

Mary Anne Clarke

Tell the air to hold me in the rushing heart of it
And keep its paths straight
Away from home let there be a land that
Flows with fish and flies
And let it taste like it tasted at home
Home take this salty scent of home from my head
Cut away the memory of its last ultraviolet
Flash beautiful beneath me
Don't turn me to a twist of salt to fall to
Sea's saltiness if I look back at my home
Let me look back just once let me
Look back

Little Birds of the Night

Stephen Crane (1871–1900)

Little birds of the night
Aye, they have much to tell
Perching there in rows
Blinking at me with their serious eyes
Recounting of flowers they have seen and loved
Of meadows and groves of the distance
And pale sands at the foot of the sea
And breezes that fly in the leaves.
They are vast in experience
These little birds that come in the night.

To the Stork

Henry Wadsworth Longfellow (1807–1882)

Welcome, O Stork! that dost wing
Thy flight from the far-away!
Thou hast brought us the signs of Spring,
Thou hast made our sad hearts gay

Descend, O Stork! descend
Upon our roof to rest;
In our ash tree, O my friend,
My darling, make thy nest.

To thee, O Stork, I complain,
O Stork, to thee I impart
The thousand sorrows, the pain
And aching of my heart.

When thou away didst go,
Away from this tree of ours,
The withering winds did blow,
And dried up all the flowers

Dark grew the brilliant sky,
Cloudy and dark and drear;
They were breaking the snow on high,
And winter was drawing near.

From Varaca's rocky wall,
From the rock of Varaca unrolled,
The snow came and covered all,
And the green meadow was cold

O Stork, our garden with snow
Was hidden away and lost,
And the rose-trees that in it grow
Were withered by snow and frost.

A Winter Bluejay

Sara Teasdale (1884–1933)

Crisply the bright snow whispered,
Crunching beneath our feet;
Behind us as we walked along the parkway,
Our shadows danced,
Fantastic shapes in vivid blue.
Across the lake the skaters
Flew to and fro,
With sharp turns weaving
A frail invisible net.
In ecstasy the earth
Drank the silver sunlight;
In ecstasy the skaters
Drank the wine of speed;
In ecstasy we laughed
Drinking the wine of love.

Had not the music of our joy
Sounded its highest note?
But no,
For suddenly, with lifted eyes you said,
"Oh look!"
There, on the black bough of a snow flecked maple,
Fearless and gay as our love,
A bluejay cocked his crest!
Oh who can tell the range of joy
Or set the bounds of beauty?

Flamingo

Cheryl Pearson

As though the gas was left on high, and a match
struck. And now the pale flames are licking at the glass

with long tongues of rosy light. Or else the yolk
of sunrise broke, and washed each bird in its blush,

the way red wine defies salt and sponge.
Some are soft; white lace held against a girl's cheek,

a peach growing down in the spring. Others blaze,
their doubles locked at a hot-pink foot.

All are exquisite. Their glad wings
sweeten the water.

The weight of it. All that beauty.
No wonder their flushed backs

sway underneath it. No wonder
the knobs of their knees are braced –

studs of colour, a bud on a branch,
the knot on the rope of a boat in the harbour.

Light as meringues. As delicate.
You describe them solely

in breakable language – eggshell, teacup,
hummingbird, wrist.

Do you think that you are capable
of grace like this? To step into cracked water,

and mend it? The vase of the throat opens.
The mouth brims with roses. How can the earth bear it?

Like love is borne; that other light
that burns, and cannot be extinguished.

The Darkling Thrush

Thomas Hardy (1840–1928)

I leant upon a coppice gate
  When Frost was spectre-gray,
And Winter's dregs made desolate
  The weakening eye of day.
The tangled bine-stems scored the sky
  Like strings of broken lyres,
And all mankind that haunted night
  Had sought their household fires.

The land's sharp features seemed to be
  The Century's corpse outleant,
His crypt the cloudy canopy,
  The wind his death-lament.
The ancient pulse of germ and birth
  Was shrunken hard and dry,
And every spirit upon earth
  Seemed fervourless as I.

At once a voice arose among
  The bleak twigs overhead
In a full-hearted evensong
  Of joy illimited;
An aged thrush, frail, gaunt, and small,
  In blast-beruffled plume,
Had chosen thus to fling his soul
  Upon the growing gloom.

So little cause for carolings
  Of such ecstatic sound
Was written on terrestial things
  Afar or nigh around,
That I could think there trembled through
  His happy good-night air
Some blessed Hope, whereof he knew
  And I was unaware.

Migrating Birds

James Thomson (1700–1748)

Where the Rhine loses his majestic force
In Belgian plains, won from the raging deep
By diligence amazing, and the strong,
Unconquerable hand of Liberty,
The stork-assembly meets; for many a day,
Consulting deep, and various, e're they take
Their plumy voyage thro' the liquid sky.
And now their rout design'd, their leaders chose,
Their tribes adjusted, clean'd their vigorous wings;
And many a circle, many a short essay
Wheel'd round and round, in congregation full,
The figur'd flight ascends; and, riding high
Th' aerial billows, mixes with the clouds.

Or where the Northern ocean, in vast whirls,
Boils round the naked, melancholy isles
Of farthest Thule, and th' Atlantic surge
Pours in among the stormy Hebrides;
Who can recount what transmigrations there
Are annual made? What nations come and go?
And how the living clouds on clouds arise?
Infinite wings! till all the plume-dark air,
And white resounding store are one wild cry

A Bird Song

Christina Rossetti (1830–1894)

It's a year almost that I have not seen her:
Oh, last summer green things were greener,
Brambles fewer, the blue sky bluer.

It's surely summer, for there's a swallow:
Come one swallow, his mate will follow,
The bird race quicken and wheel and thicken.

Oh happy swallow whose mate will follow
O'er height, o'er hollow! I'd be a swallow,
To build this weather one nest together.

The Nightingale

Margiad Evans (1909–1958)

The orchard in the valley first
the green infection took,
the birds forgot their brown highways,
the leaf forgot the root.

The butterflies on breathing wings
went by like sighs of light –
trembled the air's transparency –
articulated flight.

The mountains in the faded mists
with opening souls rejoice.
All night they heard the nightingale
in his full-moon of voice.

Credits

Pack, Clouds, Away, and Welcome Day – Thomas Heywood, from *The Rape of Lucrece*, Quarto, 1630

Ducks' Ditty – Kenneth Grahame, from *The Wind in the Willows*, 1908

The Lark's Song – William Blake, extract from *Milton* (a Poem), 1811

Azure and Gold – Amy Lowell, from *A Dome of Many-Coloured Glass*, 1912

Proud Songsters – Thomas Hardy, from *Winter Words in Various Moods and Metres*, 1928

The Windhover – Gerard Manley Hopkins, from *Poems of Gerard Manley Hopkins*, ed. Robert Bridges, 1918

Extract from The Cornish Chough – John Harris, from *A Story of Carn Brea, Essays and Poems*, 1863

Green Rain – Mary Webb, first published in *The Spectator*, 24 March 1923

Lines Written in Early Spring – William Wordsworth, from *Poetical Works*, Vol 4, 1827

The Satin Bower-bird – C. J. Dennis (Clarence Michael James Stanislaus Dennis), from *The Singing Garden*, 1935

The Woods and Banks – W. H. Davies, from *True Travellers: A Tramp's Opera in Three Acts*, 1923

Cuckoo – Anon. This modernisation from *The Ballad Literature and Popular Music of the Olden Time*, 1855

Meadowlarks – Sara Teasdale, from *Flame and Shadow*, 1920

The Birds of Paradise – John Peale Bishop, from *Green Fruit*, 1917

Humming-bird – D. H. Lawrence, from *Birds, Beasts and Flowers*, 1923

Adlestrop – Edward Thomas, from *Poems*, 1917 (Reprinted with permission from RBH Vellender on behalf of the Estate of Edward Thomas)

Flamingo – John McCullough, from *Reckless Paper Birds*, Penned in the Margins, 2019 (Reproduced with permission from Penned in the Margins)

Landscape with Vultures – Pascale Petit, from *Tiger Girl*, Bloodaxe Books, 2020 (Reproduced with permission from Bloodaxe Books)

The Ostrich – Mary E. Wilkins Freeman, from *Harper's New Monthly Magazine*, Volume 111, 1905

The Three Ravens – Anon, as found in *Country Pastimes*, Meilsamta, 1611

Repeat That, Repeat' – Gerard Manley Hopkins, from *Poems of Gerard Manley Hopkins*, ed. Robert Bridges, 1918

The Condor – Michael Hogan, from *Making Our Own Rules*, Greenfield Review Press, 1989. Copyright © 1989 Michael Hogan (Reprinted with permission of the author)

Extract from Speak, Parrot – John Skelton, from Certain Books Compiled by Master Skelton

The Kingfisher – W. H. Davies, from *To Poesy*, 1910

The Eagle – Alfred, Lord Tennyson, from *The Poetical Works of Alfred Tennyson*, Poet Laureate, 1873

The Dalliance of the Eagles – Walt Whitman, from *Leaves of Grass*, 1882

Goldfinches – John Keats, from *Poems*, 1817

Requiescat – Charlotte Mew, from *The Nation*, Volume 6, Page IX, 1910

Extract from Turkey-cock – D. H. Lawrence, from *Poetry*, November 1922

Swallows – Kathleen Jamie, from *The Tree House*, first published in 2004 by Picador, an imprint of Pan Macmillan (Reproduced by permission of Macmillan Publishers International Ltd.) Copyright © Kathleen Jamie, 2004

Extract from The Rime of the Ancient Mariner – Samuel Taylor Coleridge, *The Poetical Works of S. T. Coleridge*, ed. Henry Nelson Coleridge, 1834

In the Fields – Charlotte Mew, from *The Rambling Sailor*, 1929

Yellow Penguin – Olga Dermott-Bond (Reproduced with permission from Nine Arches Press)

The Wild Swans at Coole – W. B. Yeats, from *The Wild Swans at Coole*, 1917

Lights and Shadows – Sarah Doyle, a collage poem created from extracts of Dorothy Wordsworth's journals

Le Jardin – Oscar Wilde, from *Charmides and Other Poems*, 1913

Something Told the Wild Geese – Rachel Field, from *Branches Green*, 1934

Extract from To a Skylark – Percy Bysshe Shelley, from *Prometheus Unbound*, 1820

A Flaw – Michael Field (pen name of Katherine Bradley and Edith Cooper), from *Wild Honey from Various Thyme*, 1908

The Sand-hill Crane and Other Wild Fowl of Mexico – Isaac McLellan, from *Poems of the Rod and Gun: Or, Sports by Flood and Field*, 1886

Autumn Birds – John Clare, from *Poems Descriptive of Rural Life and Scenery*, 1821

Night Birds – Flora Cruft, from *Flora Cruft, I am a Spider Mother*, The Mum Poem Press, 2022 (Reproduced with permission from Flora Cruft)

Extract from Paradise Lost – John Milton

Sunset Wings – Dante Gabriel Rossetti, from *Ballads and Sonnets*, 1881

To the Mocking-bird – Richard Henry Wilde, from *The New Monthly Magazine and Literary Journal*, 1825

The Humming-bird – Mary Botham Howitt, from *Sketches of Natural History*, 1834

Swift by your Side – Dom Conlon, from *Out There in the Wild*, Macmillan Children's Books

Winter Bird – Katherine Mansfield, from *The New Republic*, Volumes 37–38, 1924

That's What We'd Do – Mary Mapes Dodge, from *Rhymes and Jingles*, 1881

Sweet Suffolk Owl – Thomas Vautor, from *Songs of Divers Airs and Natures*, 1619

The Arctic Tern's Prayer – Mary Anne Clarke, © Mary Anne Clarke, first published by The Poetry Society, 2013 (Reproduced with permission from Mary Anne Clarke)

Little Birds of the Night – Stephen Crane, from *The Poems of Stephen Crane*, ed. J. Katz, Cooper Square Publishers, 1966

To the Stork (Armenian popular song, from the prose version of Alishan) – Henry Wadsworth Longfellow, from *A Handful of Translations in Three Books of Song*, 1872

A Winter Bluejay – Sara Teasdale, from *Rivers to the Sea*, 1915

Flamingo – Cheryl Pearson, from *Menagerie*, The Emma Press 2020 (Reproduced with permission from The Emma Press)

The Darkling Thrush – Thomas Hardy, from *The Graphic*, 29 December 1900

Migrating Birds – James Thomson, from *The Four Seasons*, and other poems, 1735

A Bird Song – Christina Rossetti, from *Scribner's Monthly, an Illustrated Magazine for the People*, Volume 5, 1873

The Nightingale – Margiad Evans, from *A Candle Ahead*, 1956